Join Nola the Nurse® and friends as they learn all about germs. What are germs? Do they make us sick? Nola will teach in this first volume of The Germy Series, which explores germs, how to stop them, everyday heroes who fight germs, and how we can stay safe and happy.

Dr. Scharmaine Lawson has a Doctor of Nursing Practice degree from Chatham University in Pittsburgh, PA. She still maintains a busy private practice in New Orleans, Louisiana by making house calls to several elderly and disabled New Orleanians who would otherwise not receive healthcare. When this award-winning and nationally known nurse practitioner is not on the road delivering keynote speeches and various other media events, she loves reading to her two babies, Skylar Rose (10), and Wyatt Shane (7).

More info on Dr. Lawson can be found at www.DrLawsonNP.com and www.NolaTheNurse.com

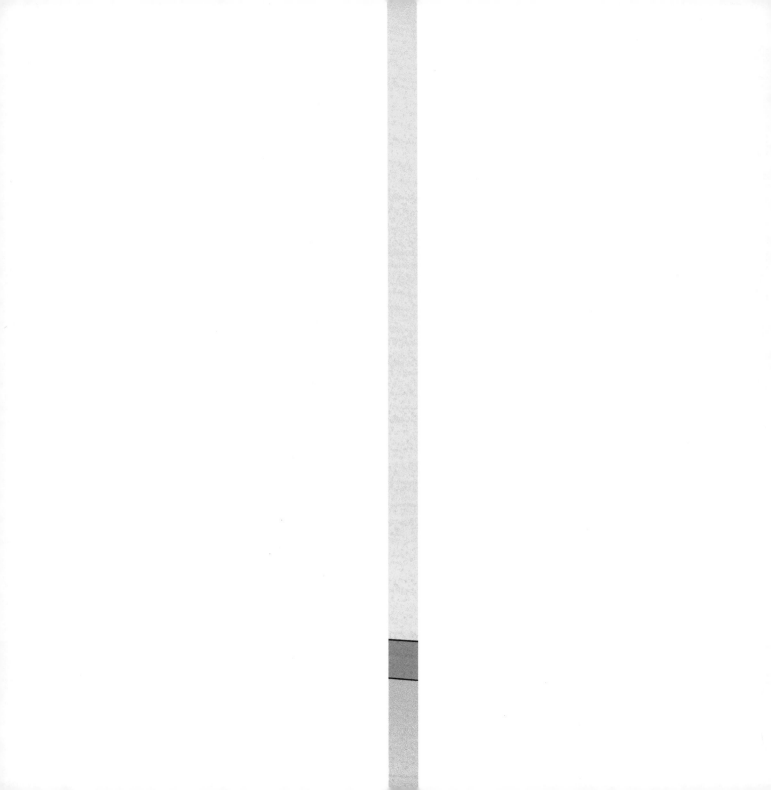

This Book Belongs to

_ _

Skylar Rose and Wyatt Shane,

thank you for allowing me to dream.
I'm a better person because
of your unconditional love.

Mommy

A DrNurse Publishing House New Orleans, Louisiana

Nola The Nurse™ Germy Series series Vol. 1

Library of Congress #: 2020910485

For information address A DrNurse Publishing House
PO Box 56572, New Orleans, La. 70152

www.NolatheNurse.com

ISBN# 978-1-945088-26-1

Author Contact info:
DrLawson@DrLawsonNP.com
www.DrLawsonNP.com

www.NolaTheNurse.com

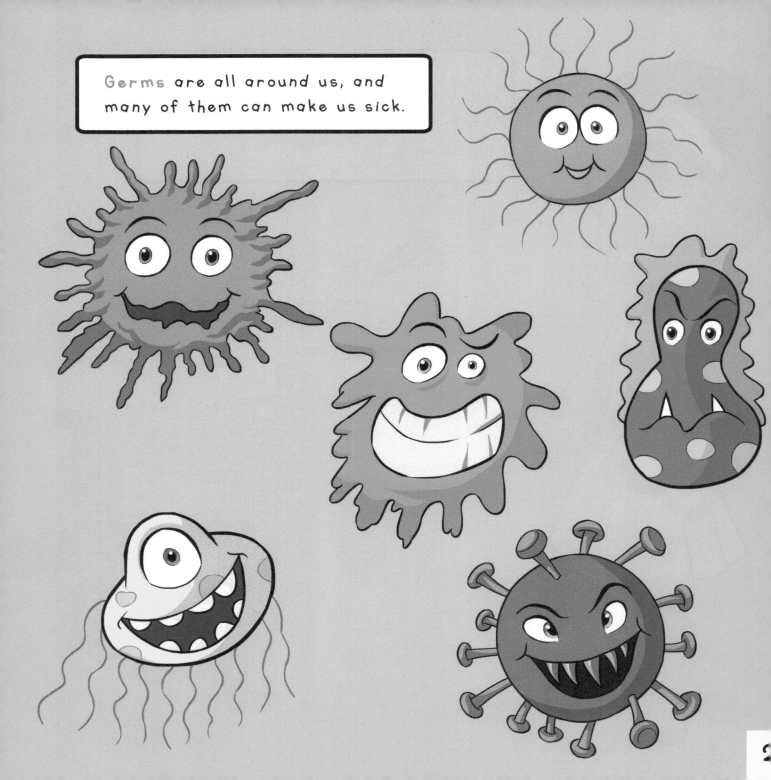

Germs are all around us, and many of them can make us sick.

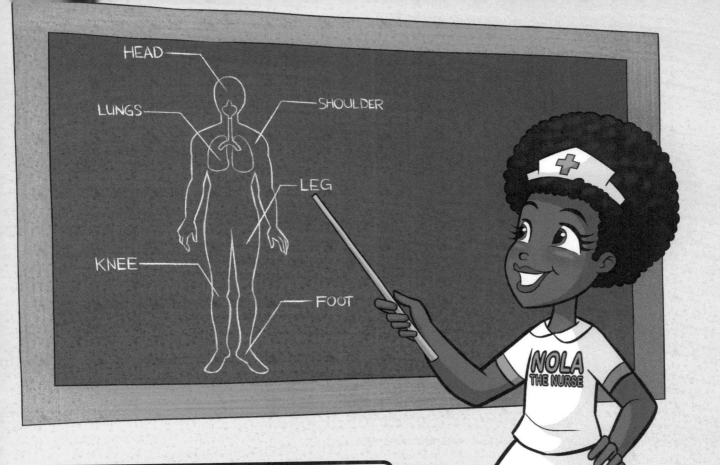

Nola is the daughter of a nurse practitioner. She has learned a lot about the human body and what makes us healthy and sick.

4

Germs are all over the place and are so very tiny. You can't see them with your eyes.

You can see them under a microscope! That's why germs are sometimes called microbes. And they are all over the place.

Oh, that's very interesting, Nola. So germs are like teeny tiny bugs that live on everything, and sometimes they make us sick.

They are on your skin, tables, chairs, and in the air. **Germs are everywhere.**

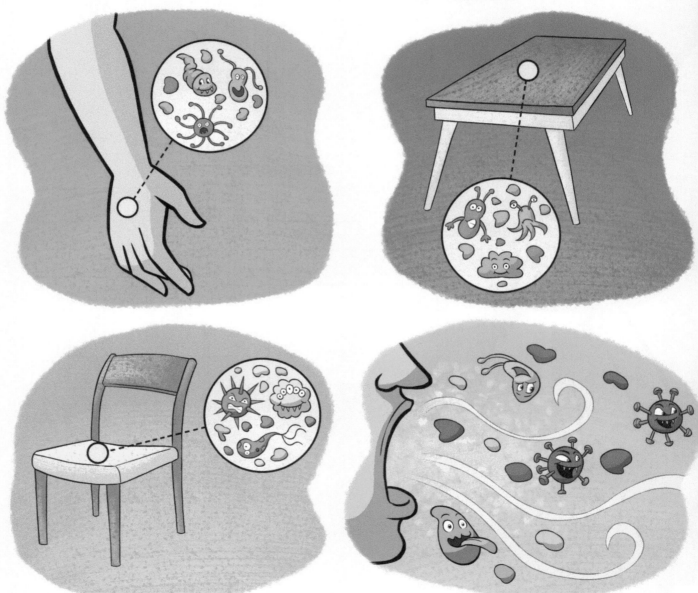

20

Nola the Nurse® loves to help people who are hurt or get sick. She learned all she knows from her mom.

1

Mom taught me that even though germs are invisible to us, they can make us really sick. **Germs can cause disease**.

11

Oh, yes! There are viruses and bacteria, but all you need to know right now is to keep yourself healthy, **you need to wash away as many germs as possible.**

Try not to touch your face before washing your hands. And cough or blow your nose on your sleeve or arm instead of your hand.

During this time of coronavirus, we can keep ourselves, our families, and friends safe by washing away germs. Can you keep clean and wash away yucky germs?

More books by Dr. Lawson

Nola The Nurse® She's On The Go Series Vol 1
Nola The Nurse® & Friends Explore The Holi Fest
She's On The Go Series Vol 2

Nola The Nurse® Activity Book for Preschool Vol 1
Nola The Nurse® Activity Book for Kindergarten Vol 2
Nola The Nurse® Math Worksheets for Kindergarten Vol 3
Nola The Nurse® English/Sight Worksheets for Kindergarten Vol 4
Nola The Nurse® Math/English Worksheets for Preschoolers Vol 5
Nola The Nurse® Math Worksheets for First Graders Vol 6
Nola The Nurse® STEM Activity Book for 5-8 year olds Vol 7

Nola The Nurse® & Friends Explore The Holi Fest
She's On The Go Series Vol 2 Coloring Book
Nola The Nurse® Remembers Hurricane Katrina
Special Edition
Nola The Nurse® Remembers Hurricane Katrina
Special Edition Coloring Book
Black Dot

www.NolaTheNurse.com
DrLawson@DrLawsonNP.com

Lightning Source UK Ltd.
Milton Keynes UK
UKHW051537260620
365570UK00004B/84